Kiln
Building

CERAMIC SKILLBOOKS

Kiln Building

Ian Gregory

Series Editor:
Murray Fieldhouse

PITMAN/WATSON GUPTILL

PITMAN PUBLISHING LIMITED
39 Parker Street, London WC2B 5PB

Associated Companies
Copp Clark Ltd, Toronto · Pitman Publishing Co. SA (Pty) Ltd,
Johannesburg · Pitman Publishing New Zealand Ltd, Wellington
Pitman Publishing Pty Ltd, Melbourne

WATSON-GUPTILL PUBLICATIONS, a division of Billboard
Publications Inc., One Astor Plaza, New York, N.Y. 10036.

First published in Great Britain 1977

© Pitman Publishing 1977

Gregory, Ian, 1942–
    Kiln building.

    (Ceramic Skillbooks)
    Includes bibliographical references and index.
    1. Kilns.   I. Title   II. Series.
TT924.G73   1977   738.1'3   77-2321

US ISBN 0-8230-0590-9
UK ISBN 0-273-01086-7 (cased edition)
UK ISBN 0-273-01001-8 (paperback edition)

Text set in 10/11 pt. IBM Century, printed by photolithography and
bound in Great Britain at the Pitman Press, Bath.

Contents

Acknowledgements

Thanks to my wife Karen for her help in writing this book, to Julie for typing, to David my assistant in kiln construction and other work around the pottery, to Vera Gregory for baby sitting. And to all those who so freely gave advice and information about their kilns: John Leach, Alan Wallwork, David Eeles, John Maltby, Peter Starkey, Peter Dick, Muffy Anderson, Ray Finch, Janet Leach, Harry Stringer and Jerome Abbo. Robin Lord for photographic advice, Cathy and Katie for re-typing and David Lewis my editor.

To the little black mouse who lives in the kiln shed and to my six children outside.

Preface

The problems of firing any ceramic kiln can be overcome with time and practice as long as the basic principles of construction have been adhered to, and the kiln has no obvious defects in design. Beginners in this field can learn a lot from building and firing various small kilns, but I must add that there is no easy short cut to this experience.

Pottery and kiln building go hand in hand and, contrary to popular belief, it is not just a case of piling bricks together, putting in a few pots, and hey presto! Producing anything with one's hands needs thought, care and application. A feeling for standards and tradition is essential and without it there is no point in continuing the art of craft pottery or the building of small pottery kilns.

Considering the limited amount of space available, I have had to keep all the necessary information concise and make references to other books where information is readily available, so as to give as much space here as possible to my own ideas. I hope to provide some ground work and general information as a starting point. I am a working potter and have written about aspects of kilns and firing that I have learnt from my own experience. There are many details that I've not gone into, but after reading this book, you will at least be able to make a start. To all kiln builders, Good Luck!

Introduction

Any potter who intends to make a living from his craft needs a
kiln which combines reliability with economy. There are already
several very informative books on the market for the would-be
kiln builder, but what I have attempted to provide in these pages
is a practical guide to the do's and don'ts of kiln building drawn
from my own experience. I believe there's a lot of truth in the old
adage 'there is no teacher like experience'!

Most of the potters I've met have spent many exhausting hours
juggling with burners and flames, coaxing their kilns to final
temperature, when the weather and other conditions are all wrong
and when an order, already overdue, was completely dependent
on a successful firing. I've looked back over kiln notes in prep-
aration for this book and am amazed at how fine the dividing line
is between a completely successful firing and a partial success: this
applies particularly when using flame as opposed to electricity,
although there are many solid fuel kilns that do fire with
accuracy and control.

I sat up most of the other night firing a salt kiln with another
potter. During our discussions we came to the conclusion that
a potter firing with wood or oil is somewhat in the position of the
old alchemist. Having made his pots, he then sets them in the kiln
and relies on the elements of earth, fire and water, plus judgement, to conjure up the end result. Whereas the oxidising electric
kiln potter is nearer the chemist who, with care and judgement,
mixes his ingredients with a much greater degree of control over
the end result.

To qualify my feelings on this aspect of potters and kilns, I
think that the following translation from Bernard Palissy gives a
far more graphic account of the problems facing the amateur, and
indeed, even a skilled maker of pots:

'Never having seen clay fired, I had no idea at what degree of heat a glaze would melt. There was, therefore, but slight chance of my succeeding, for even if my compounds had been right, my fire would have been either too hot or not hot enough. So when nothing good came out of the kiln I laid the blame on the mixtures. In the course of the first year I tried over and over again, and always failed, wasting my means and wearying myself body and soul. I had spent days and nights pounding and grinding a multitude of substances and building my own kiln at great expense of brick, wood and labour. The kiln was built in the garden at the back of my house. No sheltering wall or tree broke the force of the wind in winter, no spot could have been more bleak and comfortless. I was every night at the mercy of the wind and rain, without help or companionship, except for the owl that hooted on one side and the dogs that howled on the other. I often had nothing dry on me because of the rains that fell.'

Bernard Palissy, born in 1510 in southern France, was a painter, naturalist, surveyor, agronomist, lecturer and author of two books on nature, in which he is shown to be a precursor of Darwin. He is remembered in France as the potter who mastered the secret of glazing earthenware, and as the father of the French porcelain industry. The excerpts in this book are all from his book, *Discours Admirables* (Paris, 1580), and tell of his long struggle to obtain glaze.

1 Kiln Planning

The kilns that I have included in this book have all been chosen for their range of size, firing techniques and cost. There should be one mentioned here for more or less every circumstance and each plan can be altered to fit your own situation.

Careful consideration must also be given to cost. It would be impossible for me to do more than guess at the cost of building these kilns, as prices are constantly subject to change. The fact that many fire bricks can be bought from demolition sites and gas-works always makes it worth your while finding out about these places in your local area. I have also included various mixtures for home-made brick construction. In the long run it pays to build a kiln from the best materials you can afford. Since the life and function of your kiln should be of major concern, it is worth adding here that I built my first wood kiln, which had 100 cubic feet internal chamber capacity, for around £20 plus a great deal of detective work looking for and finding the materials second-hand.

The first thing to consider is what the kiln will be used for.

1 What kind of pottery are you going to produce:
   Earthenware?
   Stoneware?
   Saltglaze?
2 What size will the kiln be?

The size of kiln to build is governed by your circumstances. Obviously, the hobbyist will not wish to build a large kiln that takes months to fill, whereas the professional will require one of sufficient size to keep his production rate flowing smoothly. The school or college will probably need both small and large kilns; the former for testing, and the latter for firing larger pieces made by the students.

3 What space have you available to build the kiln? Is it already in an existing building or can you start from scratch? If you decide on wood or coal as fuel, have you sufficient storage space for these fuels?

4 Is your chosen site safe from the possible hazard of fire, and will the smoke or fumes bother neighbours? And do make sure no nearby trees will suffer from the exhaust heat from the chimney.

Assuming that you have decided what size kiln you want and where you are going to build it, the next step is to consider the choice of fuel. Will it be wood fired, oil, gas, coal or electric?

2 Choice of Fuels

A good starting point here is to discuss the combustion of fuel, and the use of the heat released. Flame provides a steady climb in temperature until the glazes and bodies of the pots have matured to the desired temperature. The combustion involved with the fuel (a reaction of carbonaceous matter and oxygen) and reduction capabilities are all things to consider when choosing a fuel.

Wood

It is important to know that wood, being a solid matter, can only burn on its surface area, unlike gas or liquid oil, which can be sprayed and ignited and will burn over the whole area exposed to oxygen. Wood will smoulder and ignite only on the exposed surfaces, so to get the best heat output, it follows that thinner pieces of wood will burn and release energy faster than large thick logs. This property can be used by the potter to his advantage when a slow even heat is required in the initial stages of firing and all the residual water has to be driven off before a more rapid climb in temperature can be established.

It is common sense, therefore, to keep the wood as small as possible (within practical limits) for handling and stoking, while fire boxes, ash pits and fire bars should be of generous size, and free from any area that will cause a build-up of excessive ash or charcoal. This could cut down the access for oxygen from the area of combustion and inhibit the release of the greatest amount of heat. All proportions that are shown in the plans are of adequate size for the kilns described, but it cannot be stressed enough that whenever possible, large flues and fire boxes are more efficient. Ones that are too small can prevent the required heat rise: large spaces can easily be reduced but it is difficult to enlarge chimney and flues, and sometimes this can only be done by dismantling an otherwise well proportioned kiln. It should also be noticed from the plans that because a kiln is small it doesn't necessarily follow that the combustion areas can be reduced in scale with the chamber, for obvious reasons related to heat release. Conversely, a very large kiln can be coaxed to temperature without the need of giant fire mouths.

All plans can be expanded and contracted as long as the essential ratios of chimney to flue to chamber and fire mouths are all followed with a degree of understanding of the principles involved.

Wood burning kilns have traditionally provided the chief means of firing pots in the past, and the ash deposits and flame flashes obtained are still one of the main charms of this technique. The wood burning kiln is really only a sophisticated advance from firing pots on the bonfire. By removing the direct effect of flame in the early stages and containing the heat in the more advanced stages with the use of refractory bricks, an even and controlled firing can result. The simple fire mouths described are relatively easy to build, bearing in mind the principles of construction laid out in Chapter 3.

The first thing to consider when using wood as a fuel is to decide on the type of fire mouth and size of kiln. (A wood kiln of 30—50 cubic feet consumes approximately one cord of wood. A cord of wood measures about 128 cubic feet, or a pile 8 ft x 4 ft x 4 ft: it weighs between one and one-and-a-half tons.) The earliest wood kilns used by the Chinese and Japanese were of the tunnel variety, with a fire box at the front of the chamber as in fig. 1.

Dome fire box (see fig. 2)
Sometimes known as a dutch oven fire box, this is simply a large arched chamber into which wood is stoked. The fire 'cooks' newly stoked wood with the heat radiating from the arch. This is a very efficient use of fuel, as the wood has a tendency to retain moisture even after it has been air dried for long periods. (It has been noted that 20 per cent of the moisture is retained after air drying.)

Dutch oven
Stoking a fire box using wood causes a burst of hot gases and flames to pass from the fire mouth and through the chamber, and this is why the ample flue space is required. A blow hole in some kilns is built into the crown of the chamber to allow the escape of smoke, and ensure a less carbonised atmosphere.

I have found that the lighter, more resinous timbers release their heat far more quickly than the denser hard woods. Again, you can take advantage of this property during the initial stages of warming up. Slower burning oak, for example, releases a gentle flame in the early stages, when damp or unfired pots are in danger of exploding. However, hardwoods, such as oak, birch, ash and elm yield more heat per volume than softwoods: greenwood, on the other hand, gives off only 80 percent of the available potential heat, so care should be taken to store and season fuel well before it is required for use.

Fig. 1 Early kiln design: a simple two-chamber cross-draught principle as used by the Chinese and Japanese.

Fig. 2 Side elevation of a dutch oven fire box.

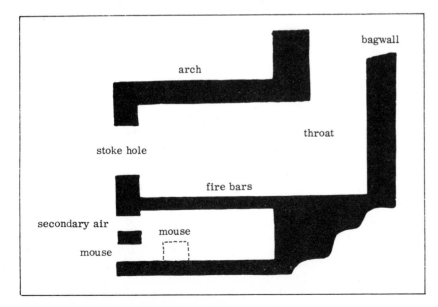

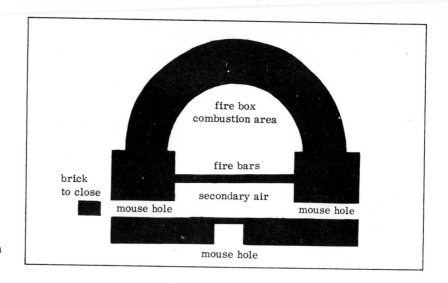

fire box
combustion area

fire bars

brick
to close

secondary air

mouse hole

mouse hole

mouse hole

Fig. 3 Front elevation of the dutch oven.

Although timber of any kind is not so easy to find as in days gone by, I have found that pine slabs give an excellent result, when really dry and seasoned. These can often be purchased quite cheaply from sawmills, although you may have to organise transport. The only disadvantage of pine slabs is that the heavy resinous bark does seem to clog up ash pits in the early stages of firing, and tends to cause slagging in the flues.

A major consideration when using wood as a fuel, is that wood kilns, because of the slow flame produced, need a large chimney to exert the right pull to draw the flames through the setting. As a rough guide: one inch of chimney width is equal to one foot of height, i.e. a chimney 18 in. across should be about 18 ft high.

Wood firings can be dirty, producing smoke, fumes and a mess of wood cuttings, and all this must be taken into consideration when choosing the site for the kiln in relation to the rest of the pottery, neighbouring houses and buildings. The storage of fuel must also be taken into account as it is essential that the timber is kept dry ready for the firing as wood can absorb moisture from the surrounding atmosphere. It is a fairly bulky material to store, and even a small kiln of 25—40 cubic feet can consume a cord of timber, (i.e. about a ton of hardwood). Therefore it follows that adequate provision must be made for storage. Wood can be dried on the roof of the kiln, as the Japanese do, but there is always the danger of it becoming ignited during the firing. An open-walled shed allowing adequate air movement is probably the best way to store wood ready for use.

The labour of continual stoking can be alleviated to a degree by the use of a self-feeding fire mouth or down-draught fire box. In the normal fire box, the primary air passes over the top of the burning fuel, but the reverse happens in the self-feeding down-draught box. As the wood burns from beneath, and the ash falls clear, the wood stacked on top drops down and continues to burn as shown in fig. 7.

This self-feeding fire mouth can be left unattended for short periods during the early stages, should it be necessary to do so, with no loss of climb in the chamber. The principle, as can be seen, is that the primary air entering the top of the fire at A pulls the flame down into the throat arch. Secondary air entering at B burns the fallen log ends and embers, which yield up at least 25—35 per cent of the calorific value of the initial stoking. This helps the kiln to fire cleanly, cutting down the amount of unburnt gases passing through the chamber. A further control comes from the mouse hole shown at C, which provides oxygen to the ash pit at its lowest point and ensures that the secondary air is preheated by the embers in the ash pit.

Wood firing

'The flame is master to the man
He controls it where he can
Should flame and man control the clay
Successful firing ends the day.'

Wood firing, although often exhausting, involves the potter with his kiln as no other fuel can do. The continual stoking and the roar of combustion, make firing a time of great excitement, and even fear! It is a very humbling experience to stand beside a reasonable sized wood kiln when it is reaching white heat. The roar of the initial stages of firing settles down to a deep-throated rumble, with tongues of flame licking from the stoke holes and iridescent heat glowing through the expansion cracks. The kiln seems to possess a life of its own as it raises itself up on its expanding brick work. It's a sight and experience not to be missed on a dark summer's night — white and cherry-red incandescent heat, sparks and flames all combining in the final act of a potter's work.

The technique of firing with wood can really only be acquired with practice. In order to gain the climb in temperature required, the fire mouth must be fed at a steady rate. If this is neglected,

Figs. 4 & 5 John Leach's wood
store. The wood is larch and
comes in bundles from a nearby
fencing company. It is cut up into
convenient lengths and left to dry
for a year, if possible: in this
length of time much of the excess
moisture disappears as the wood
is carefully stacked to allow air to
circulate.

the loss of heat will negate the climb. Over stoking will fill and choke the fire box, causing the same result, whereas steady and judicious stoking will bring about a good rise in temperature within the chamber. Flames need time to develop within the confines of fire box, throat arch and chamber; these must be watched and understood. Wood firing demands all the fireman's time, and any distraction could cause a disastrous drop in temperature. Therefore a willingness and ability to give the fire your full attention during the long firings are important. There are many unique and unpredictable bonuses that come from this medium of firing, for the delicate flashes from the flames as they brush the pots leave deposits of fly ash. These glaze the body, are aesthetically appealing, and give the potter a closeness to the final act of producing pots that no other firing method can.

There is also the added advantage with wood firing that the potter need not rely on man-made energy, and in this day and age of fuel costs, the relative cheapness of this fuel is attractive. It is worth noting that wood burns in two stages. The charring tem-

Fig. 6 John Leach has a readily available supply of peat that is used to start a wood firing. It is soaked in paraffin before being lit in the fire boxes above: it burns slowly and steadily to warm up the kiln.

11

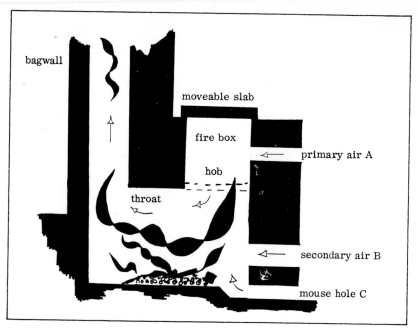

Fig. 7 Self-feeding fire box. There is a tendency for hot spots to develop in the throat arch, due to the flames pulling through the narrow throat before they spread into the ware chamber.

perature is below ignition temperature, so the first stage is really a combustion of volatile gas. The resin content of the wood adds to the heat given off at this stage and moves up into the chamber before being fully ignited where there is enough free oxygen to allow it to burn. The second stage is from the combustible charcoal, which has a higher calorific value than wood, as the hydrogen and oxygen have already burnt off. This needs oxygen to burn efficiently, and unless this is provided by the secondary air, a heap of choking 'coals' or glows will build up in the fire box. The localised heat given off by the burning charcoal is often the reason for badly warped fire bars and fire mouth breakdown.

Historically, wood has been used as a kiln fuel by almost all cultures. The length of wood flame can be very dramatic when seen to travel from fire box to chimney top — in excess of 26 ft in my kiln. This can be produced by a single stoking of a piece of wood 2 in. x 2 in. x 18 in. Its advantage over other solid fuel is that there is little residue left in the fire box. It would seem from the hardness and refractory quality of the ash left after a stoneware firing that the extreme heat, as with salt in the salt firing, volatises the alkalis in ash, changing the ash from its usual light nature to this denser granular texture. A final point to note is that the fly ash will leave a deposit of glaze on the interior of the chamber and shelves. Pot lids and shelf tops should be coated with batwash to avoid sticking. Cones may melt earlier than their true temperature due to added flux from this ash.

See Michael Cardew's *Pioneer Potter* for a full description of a wood firing procedure, and Bernard Leach's *A Potter's Book* for full details of an up-draught wood kiln.

Gottlieb figures on wood burning

Type of wood	Calories	B.T.U.
Pine	5085	9153
Fir	5035	9053
Beech	4774	8591
Birch	4771	8586
Elm	4728	8510
Ash	4711	8480
Oak	4620	8316

Oil

Oil is one of the main fuels used today for kiln firing by the craft potter. The amount of information available on the subject is very comprehensive, so I shall refer you to Daniel Rhodes' book on *Kilns* for general detail and try to fill in here the more basic information needed to set up using this fuel.

As a fuel, oil produces good results, in that the atmosphere can be fairly well controlled from reduction to clear oxidation, and a steady advance in temperature maintained. The oil flame itself tends to cause slagging in the fire box, so care must be taken when fire mouths are built, that the bricks are of the right quality, able to withstand the intense harsh flame, and are of adequate size to allow for complete combustion.

The principle used in getting oil to burn effectively is to break it up into droplets by two methods. This can be done by the drip type of burner as shown in fig. 8.

Drip plate burner
This is made from a 6 in. square steel tube by 1 ft long, with plates welded as shown. The dripping oil falls on to the flash plate and ignites, falling, if unburnt, on to a second plate. Air passing from the front of the tube completes combustion, but as in the case of many of these types of burner, during the initial heating-up stage, a great deal of smoke and fumes are created. Once hot, their performance is improved considerably.

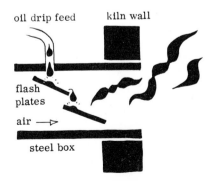

Fig. 8 A drip plate burner.

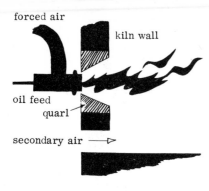

Fig. 9 Spraying oil with air.

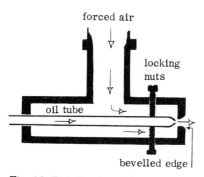

Fig. 10 Details of an oil burner.

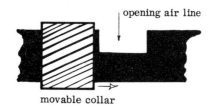

Fig. 11 Movable collar on the air pipe that allows control over the pressure at which the air is delivered to the burner.

A far more efficient system of burning oil is to break it up into fine droplets or spray which can be easily ignited and which gives a very controllable flame. Oil is fed, as in the drip burner, from a gravity tank. The air is supplied under pressure. Thus, the two can be combined together to form a spray. Secondary air is also pulled in around the cone-shaped fire mouth or quarl and combustion takes place.

Fine adjustment of air and oil produce a controlled flame. This burner can be constructed from basic pipe fittings as follows:

Air is supplied from a vacuum cleaner at a steady pressure through 2 in. or $2\frac{1}{2}$ in. hose. The burner is made from a T-shaped piece of iron pipe of the same bore as the air hose. The oil is fed from a gravity tank to a pipe of brass or steel, whose outside diameter is $\frac{3}{8}$ in., flattened at the delivery end to give a nozzle about $\frac{1}{32}$ in. by $\frac{3}{8}$ in. This nozzle is formed by flattening the oil pipe and filing it to give a bevelled edge. A corresponding horizontal slot is cut in the centre of the cap by drilling $\frac{3}{8}$ in. holes at $\frac{1}{2}$ in. centres and cutting between them. Two threaded bolts hold the oil pipe in the correct position and allow for jet adjustment (see fig. 10).

Oil burner
Provided the vacuum cleaner is powerful enough, a larger diameter oil pipe can be used. The burner can be made more efficient by drilling two tiny holes at the back of the air opening in the nozzle and in either side. These must be bevelled in the same manner as the main outlet at the back.

The disadvantages of home-made burners are many. The control over the fuel and air mixture is not necessarily very precise and does not give optimum use of fuel. This can be overcome to a certain extent by cutting a U-shaped wedge out of the plastic tube leading to the vacuum cleaner and putting a collar over the hole. Should the amount of air passing through the nozzle be too great, then the collar can be eased back to release some of the pressure before it reaches the burner head (see fig. 11).
The oil can be adjusted back at the same time. This control will be of great use during the early stages of firing when the fire boxes are cold and insufficient combustion produces the well-known clouds of black smoke so often seen in the early stages of firing with oil when using primitive burner systems. (See Rhodes, page 74 for a description of a similar burner.)

One disadvantage with this type of burner, even in the more sophisticated oil systems, is that it tends to be difficult to light in the early stages when both fire mouth and brickwork are cold. This tendency can be overcome by placing a bent wire in front of the nozzle; this wire, once hot, will re-ignite the oil should it go out. See fig. 12.

Another method is to have a wick beside the burner (see fig. 13) reaching back into a small can of oil. This should re-ignite the main spray if it goes out.

Jet burners pass enough air to atomise the fuel but often do not give enough for full combustion at peak flow. A balance comes from the control of secondary air pulled in around the burner nozzle and supplied in the usual fashion through the air inlet under the quarl. The chimney plays an important role, just as in the wood kiln, by pulling the flame through the chamber. The effective size is obviously therefore just as critical for a successful firing, with oil as with solid fuel.

Oil flames produce severe conditions in the fire box and the limited heat pattern and growth outward from localised heat has a tendency to cause expansion stresses on this area of the kiln. It is wise to place loose bricks at the back of the fire mouth to bear the brunt of the flame and protect the end wall of the chamber (see fig. 14).

In spite of the drawbacks there are many good reasons for using these simple burners, the most obvious being their low cost, especially when compared with manufactured equipment.
To sum up, oil as a fuel gives good controlled results from oxidation to reduction. A rapid advance of heat can be achieved relatively easily once the kiln has warmed up and the fire mouths are hot. The fuel is easily stored near the kiln site and takes up little space. The usual fire precautions should be carefully observed, however, and regular checks made on all pipe work around the kiln, especially before and during firing.

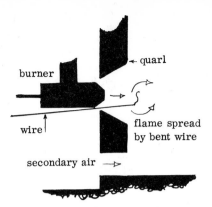

Fig. 12 A piece of bent wire pushed in front of the nozzle that will re-ignite in the early stages of a firing if fire mouths are cold.

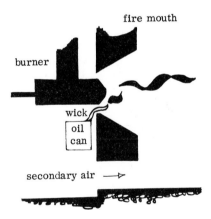

Fig. 13 Alternative method of ensuring ignition: a wick placed beside the burner.

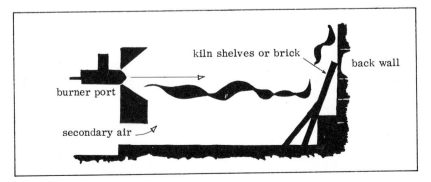

Fig. 14 Loose bricks or old shelves put at the back of the chamber to protect the structure from extremely intense heat.

Coal and coke

Coal has been widely used as a kiln fuel for many years. Many of the now defunct bottle kilns were fired in this way with several fire boxes around the sides of the chamber. Coal has one drawback in that it releases a great deal of sulphurous gas which can have damaging effects on some glazes, but its ability to release a great deal of heat in relation to its size cannot be discounted, and it seems an ideal medium for firing the small kiln, especially for raku, where a steady temperature must be maintained during the glazing period.

As a fuel for large kilns, I think its storage space, inevitable dirt and expense, rather puts coal to the bottom of the fuel list for practical reasons. I have, however, included a coal kiln plan later in the book.

Toward the end of the firing it is usually only necessary to stoke from time to time to avoid overloading and choking the fire box, while keeping the fires burning steadily without cooling and clinkering up. Use a bent steel rod to clear clinker from between fire bars. The spaces between fire bars should be 1 in. to $1\frac{1}{2}$ in. for bituminous coal. Bars $1\frac{1}{4}$ in. to $1\frac{1}{2}$ in. square steel are necessary and even these will have to be removed to be bent straight again, or reversed, if they bend badly due to the intense white heat. Fire bars made from iron frequently need replacing due to the high ember temperature of coal and this can prove a costly nuisance.

The lack of reliance on electricity for power is one of the advantages of solid fuel fired kilns, with the added bonus of the fly ash effects and the fuel's ability to fire both oxidised and reduced atmospheres.

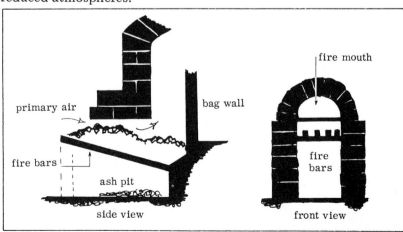

Fig. 15 A coal burning fire box, side and front views.
As in the case of wood firing, adequate space must be allowed for the entry of oxygen to keep a strong fire burning.

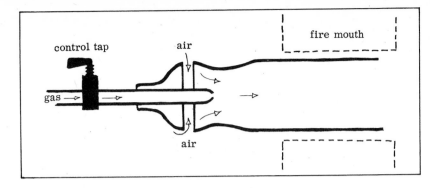

Fig. 16 Simple gas burner.

Gas

Should gas be available, then obviously you will have no fuel
storage problems as you can connect up to the mains. It is a
relatively safe and simple way of firing. As with oil, there are
several manufactured burners available, but with a little time using
basic tools, burners can be made from standard pipe fittings.

Simple gas burner
An iron tube forms the body of the burner. A narrow pipe fitted
with a tap to control the gas flow passes into the body as shown
in fig. 16. As the gas flows through the body it pulls air in at
opening A. The air and gas combine and are ignited at the nozzle.
The narrow taper just in front of the outlet causes a constriction
and speeds the flow of gas which helps to suck air in from behind.

This simple system may burn back within the tube but this can
be overcome by adjusting the air intake at the back until the
correct balance is obtained. Oxidising and reduction can be controlled with comparative ease and a very low or a long, fast flame
can be developed accordingly by turning up and down the gas
supply. In Daniel Rhodes' *Kilns* book, several variations on this
theme for simple venture burners are shown, so I refer you to
that chapter for further detail.

Of course, natural gas is not the only gas available. Propane or
bottled gas can be used in the same way, but the cost of this form
of fuel for kiln firing is very high.

Should gas be your choice of fuel then do ask for help from
your local Gas Board as they will advise on what you will need in
fittings and the cost of it all, a very important factor to consider
before going ahead.

3 Kiln Type and Size

In my opinion, the first points to consider before building a kiln are:

1 Size and shape
2 Temperature requirements
3 Chimney space and height
4 Fuel
5 Fire hazards
6 Cost
7 Size and type of ware to be fired
8 Kiln performance

1 Size and shape

A small kiln may be all that is required by a hobby pottery or a small school, but for production work it may incur too much packing and unpacking, thus consuming too much of the potter's working time.

Secondly, a small kiln uses considerably more fuel in relation to the number of pots fired than a larger one. The initial heating of brickwork etc., once achieved, is balanced out in a larger kiln with the extra packing space. The smaller kiln is not so economical, although a small chamber can be fired repeatedly by using residual heat left behind by each consecutive load of pots.

Larger kilns usually have longer intervals between firing and also any failure can be disastrous in the quantity of losses. Too small a kiln, on the other hand, can mean a restriction on the size of ware produced and on general freedom of working. But the small kiln is very useful for testing glazes quickly and helps to maintain a feeling of 'flow' in the making process from clay to finished pot.

The next factor in deciding the size and shape of the kiln is whether to build one that is up-draught or down-draught.

Up-draught

This shape kiln is really an extension of the bonfire or chimney system and has been used by many nations for centuries with great success. The fire is lit at the bottom of the chamber, travels up through a chequer system in the floor and passes through the ware and out at the top. Up-draught kilns need less burner capacity than down-draught kilns.

One drawback of this type of kiln is its habit of developing 'chimneys' within the chamber. These are areas where the flame path concentrates between pots and finds the most natural path upwards. These 'chimneys' become very hot and the pots can be badly over-fired in consequence. Other areas of the chamber will be under-fired as the heat has been pulled away from them. Allowances can be made for this by judicious packing in the chamber. The other tendency in this simple kiln shape is for the floor area always to be hotter than the top, again causing un-eveness in temperature.

Down-draught

The down-draught kiln works on the principle that heat is introduced from the fire box and the flames are deflected upward by a bagwall into the chamber, down through the pots and out through a flue in the floor. The flames go out through the chimney, or into a second chamber before leaving the back of the kiln.
This type of kiln is far more efficient than the up-draught kiln. It

Fig. 17 *Left*: The up-draught bottle kiln principle.
  Above: The down-draught kiln.
Right: The cross-draught kiln.

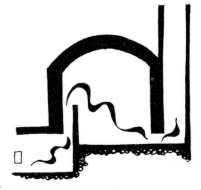

tends to fire more evenly, since the flames are held in the chamber for a greater length of time, and the added control of a damper in the chimney allows for adjustment of chimney pull and therefore of kiln atmosphere.

2 Temperature requirements

This is a simple matter of deciding whether you want to produce raku, earthenware, stoneware or saltglaze pottery. The different temperature requirement of each technique gives the answer to this question.

3 Chimney space and height

Consider the building that the kiln is to be housed in; if it is already in existence, then you must decide where a chimney would be best placed in order to clear the roof timbers, and whether smoke may affect your neighbours and nearby trees.

4 Fuel

The previous chapter deals with the advantages and disadvantages of different fuels. You should also plan where the fuel can be stored. For example, in the case of oil, a gravity tank and bulky storage tank will have to be conveniently sited.

5 Fire hazards

What is the building made of and what dangers of fire are there? Make sure that all plumbing and pipework is jointed well, and securely: pools of oil and combustible materials spell disaster, not only for the potter and his home, but possibly for everyone else nearby! A fire extinguisher is a must.

6 Cost

What can you afford? Always make the best job your purse will stretch to, as it will pay dividends over the years. It may be possible to find disused kiln bricks from old gasworks and foundries if you wish to save some expense.

7 Size and type of ware to be fired

This obviously governs the sort of kiln you need, especially if large pieces are planned, or if saltglazing techniques are to be employed.

8 Kiln performance

Frequency of firings, temperature, reduction or oxidation — these are all factors to consider. Firing time means the length of a firing — are you going to be able to stay with the kiln (and awake!) during the complete cycle?

Kiln proportions and design

These are the points to consider when deciding kiln proportions:

1 Good circulation in the chamber
2 Ample burner and fire box
3 Adequate flue size
4 Sufficiently large chimney for draught

Kiln design

The details of plans included in the text are not based on very specific measurements, but rather on the rule of thumb principle. It has been said that a supposedly bad kiln can be coaxed to temperature by a good fireman and indeed, in the early days, journeying kiln firers travelled the countryside from workshop to workshop firing kilns for the potters. In Japan too, kiln firing is a difficult and exacting task done by a few skilled members of the community. There are, however, several basic rules to consider when designing kilns to acquire the necessary temperatures for a glaze firing. These rules are the result of practical experience from past kiln building and calculations from basic principles.

The more obvious compact cubic shape will prove to have advantages over a long, low structure, or a tall, narrow one. The latter should only be considered if one is specialising in a ware that requires a kiln built to accommodate it. The more evenly proportioned kiln will probably fire more successfully because of the temperature soak radiating heat from one pot to another in a compact setting. This is a factor of great importance for good finished results. The soaking process at the completion of a firing ensures that all the wares receive a good overall temperature.

Chamber

Considering the number of various shapes and sizes of kilns that have been built and fired efficiently, it would seem that as long as a few basic rules are followed, any shape will work. What the finished pots look like is a different matter. An evenly fired chamber from top to bottom takes thought in design and building. A simple cube shape seems best, both from the packing

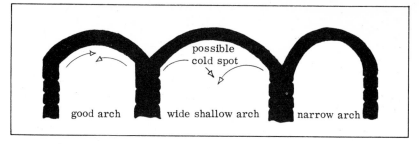

Fig. 18 Arches: keep a simple curve that is not too shallow or too tight.

point of view and for ease of firing evenly. But as long as you follow these fundamental rules, you can branch out with your own design.

Bernard Leach, in *A Potter's Book*, notes that the height and width should be approximately equal. The ratio between superficial grate areas and kiln floor governs the normal working temperature 900°C—1000°C = 1 sq ft of grate to 8 sq ft of floor; 1300°C or over = 1 sq ft of grate to 4 sq ft of floor.

The arch is best built in a simple curve rather than in an exaggerated one, since a very deep vaulted crown may cause uneven flame patterns and subsequent cold spots.

The fire boxes should give adequate heat to provide the necessary temperature climb. A grate ratio of 1 sq ft of grate to 4 sq ft of kiln floor is about right for stoneware, although this can be enlarged without any loss of firing ability to 1 sq ft of grate to 6 sq ft of floor with solid fuel.

Gas, for example, needs approximately 500 cubic centimetres ahead of it in which to burn, that is, $4\frac{1}{2}$ in. to $5\frac{1}{2}$ in. from inside kiln wall to bagwall.

Oil needs more space than gas and a trough long enough for flame development: a trough of say, 8 in. x 8 in. x 2 ft long minimum. And wood needs even more space than oil to allow for complete combustion.

The flue and chimney should be of good proportions and, where possible, allowance made for changing the size of these. As mentioned earlier the height of the chimney is governed by various factors in width and kiln size. The greater the height of the chimney, the greater the pull. A general rule for the chimney height required to induce the correct draught is 1 in. of stack width = 1 ft of stack height; a chimney, say, 18 in. wide would thus require a height of approximately 18 ft. Don't forget the horizontal pull when calculating this dimension, as allowance must also be made for this; each foot of cross-draught (horizontal pull) needs two feet of chimney height, in addition to the vertical pull. The imperial rule is, 1 ft of vertical chimney for every $3\frac{1}{2}$ ft of horizontal draught. Chimney diameter should always be at least equal to that of the flue and, if anything, on the larger side. This slight difference in flue to chimney ratio can help develop a faster movement of gases at the chimney base. Any down-draught kiln needs a strong enough draught to clear the hot gases and flame through the chamber.

So, it is far better to be generous when calculating height and width. A chimney that narrows toward the top will help induce a strong natural draught and reduce atmospheric pressure, but care must be taken when deciding on these factors, since a chimney that induces too strong a pull may cause irregular heating, as the flame may be drawn through the setting too quickly. The use of a damper to restrict chimney pull can help control the speed of a flame through the kiln.

The flue is better made over-large, since it can be easier to reduce the size than having to cut bricks out to enlarge it. The dimensions are dependent on the type of fuel to be used. An average ratio of, say, 30 to 40 cu ft of packing space would need a flue size of 9 sq in. All these measurements can be modified according to your own needs, and no hard and fast rules can be laid down.

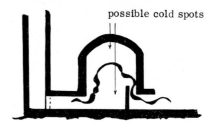

possible cold spots

Fig. 19 Too tall a chimney means too much pull and results in cold spots in these places.

4 Materials

The first thing to consider when deciding on materials for kiln building is the type of ware to be fired. Should your choice be low-fired earthenware or raku, then there are several materials suitable for the purpose that will withstand temperatures of 900°C–1000°C, for example, common house bricks, or any combination of sand and earthenware clay. The second consideration is the cost of the kiln — an important factor when choosing building materials — since the highly refractory materials become progressively more expensive as their heat duty rating increases. A fire brick that will suffice for temperatures around 1100°C to 1250°C is quite cheap, whereas a high heat duty insulating brick can cost much more. Also, the fuel which is going to be used to fire the kiln affects the choice of materials in the construction.

A fire mouth should always be built from the best bricks you can afford, since this is one part of the chamber that really has to stand up to a great deal of stress and strain. Therefore, it always pays to invest in good material, for continual repair and rebuilding can become a nuisance. All the kilns that I describe in the following pages are designed to withstand constant use and should, with understanding and judgement, produce the results required of them, as long as they are built from suitable bricks.

Solid fire brick

Solid fire bricks are made basically from fire clay and grog, fired to cone 10 upwards. They are hard, dense, volume stable and graded according to their capacity to withstand various temperatures, their physical properties and their chemical composition. Any of the manufacturers will gladly supply details and give advice on which of their brick types are best for a particular kiln. It is unnecessary for me to go into further details on this subject as each manufacturer has his own grading system. Let it suffice to say that the better the quality of brick, the longer working life it has, and it is worth the initial expense for the time saved on repairs.

It must be noted that for a salt kiln, highly siliceous fire bricks attract more sodium than those with a high alumina content: porous brick and insulation brick absorb sodium easily. The high alumina and low iron brick with a relatively hard face is better for a salt kiln. The main point to remember is that the deterioration of refractories is much faster in a salt kiln than in a normal stoneware kiln.

A solid fire brick soaks up heat and takes longer to cool than a high temperature insulating brick. Thus, more heat is used in raising the temperature of a kiln made of this solid mass. It must also be taken into account that there is a heat loss if the walls are insufficiently insulated. This is a factor worth noting when deciding which materials to build with: another point to remember is that these solid bricks have a longer working life and better resistance to slag attack and spalling.

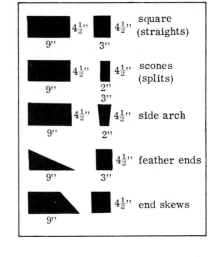

Fig. 20 Different brick shapes and sizes.

Advantages

Relative cheapness.
Ability to withstand high temperatures.
Their dense nature means that they tend to last for a considerable time, even under a heavy workload.
Their heat retention is good for radiated heat soak at top temperature and slow cooling.

Disadvantages

Difficult to cut.
Their weight and lack of insulating properties mean that they are not very economic on fuel.
A back-up of insulation is essential.

The desirable properties of any fire bricks are their strength, good refraction, and ability to withstand heat work, especially high heat duty. High alumina brick is best for salt kilns, the less iron in the bricks the better. Sillimanite or fused alumina bricks are the very best for this purpose. Their resistance to wear and abrasion makes them an ideal material for building door jambs and arches, as this is where there is always the possibility of a spalled surface falling down on to the pots below. Fire bricks are always of a well-graded, practical size.

Common bricks

If a kiln is only going to be used for low temperature firing, common house bricks may be used. The more sandy and open their structure the better, as this type of brick will withstand the thermal shock of being repeatedly heated and cooled much better than a dense engineering brick, which tends to crack and split under stress.

In the *Potter's Book*, Bernard Leach describes his raku kiln built from common bricks which was fired over one hundred times with no ill effects. Another use for house bricks in kiln building is as an additional skin built around the fire brick structure. Between these two layers a fill of insulating material is sandwiched (see insulation section). This also gives added protection from the weather conditions of the kiln is sited outside. Common bricks can also be used in the upper part of the chimney, where it is unnecessary to use solid fire bricks.

Hot face insulating bricks

Hot face insulating bricks, as their name implies, can be used for interior wall building. They are made from fire clay and kaolin, mixed with air in thick slip. This gives them a cellular composition like that of a natural sponge. The trapped air bubbles give these bricks their good insulating qualities and the body mix enables them to withstand high temperatures. Further advantages of these hot face insulators is that the kiln construction is much lighter in weight: this is very useful should the kiln have a removable top. They are easy to cut using a simple bow saw; so they can be shaped to fit any odd angle and can be drilled and cut to make spy holes and other small apertures in the chamber or door. The cost is higher than for a solid fire brick, but the saving on fuel from their insulating ability makes them the most popular material for commercial and craft potter alike. They do tend, however, to break down faster than solid fire bricks; due to their soft composition they chip and spall easily. These hot face bricks should not be used in fire mouth building or door jambs, nor will they withstand a salt attack; and they only last one or two firings in a salt kiln, as I found out to my cost! For further information see Daniel Rhodes' chapter on kiln bricks in his book *Kilns*.

Castables

Refractory concrete can be used to cast various parts of the kiln structure, either *in situ*, or separately and built in later. All the usual brick shapes can be made, such as wedges and skew backs, or it can be used for the arch. It can also be used as a mass when casting the walls or the crown of the chamber in one piece. Most calcium aluminate castables will withstand 1300°C, but the coarser iron-containing grade of *ciment fondu* will not exceed 1250°C without the addition of grog. The large amount of iron in *ciment fondu* makes it impractical for high heat duty, especially in a salt kiln where a higher alumina cement is better for the job. Again, should you wish to use this material for your kiln, it would be wise to contact the manufacturers and ask their advice.

Castable concrete is easy to use as long as care is taken in following the mixing instructions. Failure to do this can produce weak and dangerous surfaces. The aggregate is mixed with water as with normal Portland cement, and poured into a mould or shuttering, allowing 24 hours for setting. The structure or blocks can then be fired slowly up to the maximum recommended temperature. One drawback with castable refractory is that the face exposed to the interior of the kiln will fire higher than the area away from the heat. This can cause a zone of weakness to develop in the block, as shown in the diagram.

After many firings this can, and does, cause the block to spall away or split and part along this zone. The trouble can be over-come by pre-firing cast pieces in another kiln up to the optimum heat required of the blocks. This will eliminate the zone, as the block will be fired right through and therefore stabilised. Of course, large areas cannot be treated in this way. However, an arch could be sectioned, so that each piece could be fired before building, as shown in fig. 22.

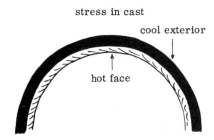

Fig. 21 A zone of weakness in a cast arch between inside and out-side face.

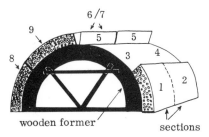

Fig. 22 Diagram of a sectioned arch. The arch is cast in sections: 3 and 4 are yet to be cast; 5 is the key section that locks the others in position.

Advantages	*Disadvantages*
Flexibility in building any part of the chamber.	Development of zones of weakness in monolithic castings.
Ability to withstand high heat duty.	No insulating qualities.
	Cannot easily be taken out and re-used, unless in block form.
	In the case of high alumina type cement, very expensive.

Insulation

Any kiln can be used and fired without insulation, especially when only low temperatures are reached, as the amount of fuel wasted is fairly negligible. In the case of high heat work, in the stoneware temperature range, it seems only common sense in these days of fuel economy to take care to use every possible method to make the kiln efficient and light on fuel.

There are many types of insulating bricks on the market which will give great fuel savings when used around solid fire brick structures. These are invariably supplied by the same manufacturers as solid fire brick and hot face bricks. Alternatively, a kiln can be covered with a layer of chopped straw or sawdust, mixed with ball clay and sand in a ratio of two to three. During firing the carbonaceous material will slowly burn out, leaving this outer skin filled with small air gaps. This will give a surface much the same as a manufactured insulation brick. Michael Cardew suggests sawdust 50, kaolin 40, ball clay 10 as a mix for insulation.

Vermiculite

This is relatively cheap and can be either poured as a loose fill between the inside wall and the outside skin to give a layer of insulation, or as a mixture (as with clay and sawdust), it can be trowled over the whole chamber. The addition of sodium silicate will help to bind the ingredients and provide dry strength when in position.

70 parts vermiculite

15 ball clay

} Plus sodium silicate

Vermiculite is not very refractory, so it must not be used near the hot face. The chopped straw and fire clay mixed is better for this purpose, should it be needed.

$$\left.\begin{array}{l}\text{3 parts sawdust} \\ \text{1 part fire clay} \\ \text{1 part ball clay}\end{array}\right\}\ \text{plus sodium silicate}$$

Remember that fire bricks can be cast from this mix.

Diatomaceous earth

This can be used in the same way as vermiculite or as a fill between the inside kiln wall with, for example, a layer of asbestos board outside. It is a very good way of providing insulation for a small kiln, since asbestos can be cut and braced in an angle iron framework.

Aluminium foil

This, used as a layer between hot face and insulation brick, or fill, will help to reflect radiated heat back towards the chamber and give an added fuel saving.

There would seem to be no way of fully containing the heat inside a kiln chamber by use of insulating materials, but they certainly do help to cut down on heat wastage through kiln walls and help to make raw fuel burning kilns a more practical proposition.

5 Construction

I have broken this chapter down into the following sections in order to work through the whole structure step by step.

1 Foundations
2 Fire box
3 Floor and walls ⎫
4 Crown and arches ⎬ Brick and castable
5 Insulation ⎭
6 Damper slots and flue box
7 Chimney
  Iron work and extras

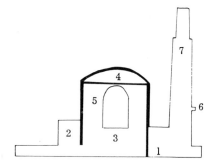

Fig. 23 Principle areas dealt with in construction.

1 Foundations

Indoors, the kiln should have a reinforced concrete foundation 3 to 4 in. thick with a waterproof membrane. In a small kiln it can be brought up to a reasonable height for loading by building the structure on a raised dias of concrete cavity block.

Outdoors, footings are needed beneath the concrete slab to give frost protection, as with any other building structure. There must be a damp-proof membrane of polythene covered with aluminium foil and 5 to 6 in. of concrete, to prevent moisture from rising up into the brickwork by capillary action. Unless care is taken to provide a barrier between the damp ground and the kiln floor, considerable fuel will be wasted drying off the moisture at the commencement of each firing.

Bernard Palissy too had a problem:

> 'But now occurred a fresh calamity, possibly the most serious that had yet befallen me, I ran out of fuel! I burned the palings of the fence around my garden. When all these were consumed I added to the fire our tables and

chairs. Then I burned the floor of our house, in the hope of melting the mixture.'

Be warned!

One good method recommended by Michael Cardew in *Pioneer Pottery* is to dig a pit and fill this with flints about fist size. These will act as a damp-proof barrier, with a layer of levelled-off common bricks on top acting as a bed on which the floor can be laid down.

Bricklaying

The line of bricks should be laid so that none of the joints are above each other. As in normal house building each course overlays the next. This is also true of a double wall. Make a point of keeping joints covered by the next layer from inner to outer courses.

Mortar

The best mortar for laying the brickwork is made from mixing clay and sand, or grog, in a ratio of two parts clay to one part sand. This mix has an advantage over the manufactured cements in that it is easy to remove from brickwork, should the kiln be dismantled for any reason. The cheapness of this material is also an advantage.

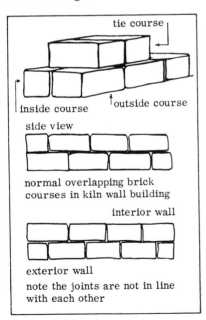

Fig. 24 Bricklaying.

tie course

inside course | outside course

side view

normal overlapping brick courses in kiln wall building

interior wall

exterior wall

note the joints are not in line with each other

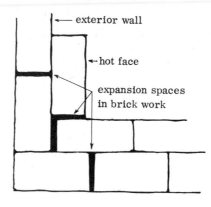

Fig. 25 Expansion gaps to be left when laying a course of bricks.

The mixture of clay and sand is better used as a thick cream; the bricks should be dampened before applying, so that the moisture is not sucked from the mixture, thus preventing its adhesion.

The most important factor in kiln brickwork is to keep each course level and straight. Allowance should be made in the structure for expansion, as the kiln is going to move and swell with the heat. This allowance is made by providing gaps here and there in a course of bricks. A gap of $\frac{1}{4}$ in. to $\frac{1}{2}$ in. left between every tenth brick in a course is sufficient.

A kiln built with a very tight construction may look beautiful before firing, but will bulge and distort after several heatings and coolings. It always pays to build all four walls (working round course by course) at one go, so that the structure doesn't develop a lean during its construction.

2 Fire box

External fire boxes should be insulated against heat loss and built of a suitably strong material to withstand high temperatures. The use of an internal grate means that although the chamber space is lost for packing pots, all heat is contained inside the kiln. The external grate loses valuable heat through its crown and brickwork before moving into the setting. Brickwork and mortar are laid in the same way as any other part of the construction.

3 Floor and walls

Don't forget always to build in brick multiples wherever possible, to avoid unnecessary cutting. A double brick wall can have tie

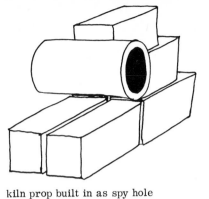
kiln prop built in as spy hole

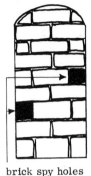
brick spy holes

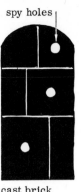
spy holes

cast brick
section for door

Fig. 26 Different ways of building in spy holes.

courses at various levels to keep the structure firmly linked together from the inside course to the outer. Hot face and insulating bricks should not be tied across in this way for obvious reasons, but it is a good idea to lay both walls as you go. In the case of common bricks, which are smaller than fire bricks, the extra can be made up with excess mortar.

Always establish corners with care, and use a builder's line to keep the brickwork true, checking the level as you go. When half bricks are needed, score the brick all round, including the four corners, and then cut across the scored line with a brick chisel. Cutting on a bed of sand helps to prevent splitting. In the case of soft H.T. bricks a bow saw can be used, but they are very abrasive and saw blades quickly wear out. Carborundum discs can be used and may save time and money if you have a power saw available. Don't forget that a loose, but not too casually built structure is better than a tight one.

The door, or wicket as it is called, should not be in the walls supporting the crown. Again, this should be measured in brick multiples, since it will be bricked in before each firing. It should be of generous size for ease of loading and the jambs should be made from good hard brick.

Spy holes can be built into the brickwork at the sides of the door or at any other convenient point. A 12 in. prop mortared into the wall is a convenient method of doing this. Most draw trial holes and spies are probably better placed in the door, and bricked in before each firing, as the position of cones, shelves, etc., varies with each setting.

Cast blocks can be used, if made to measure in fewer pieces than bricks, to save time when bricking up the door.

4 Crown and arches

Small arches, flue exits for example, can be dealt with by simply corbelling over the gap, or by casting a long block to bridge the gap. The main arch is not quite such a simple job, but brick manufacturers will tell you the number and type of bricks you require for any given arch measurements.

A former will be needed in order to construct the arch in the correct position on the walls. This is best made from wood with hardboard laid over it. Cut two or three templates for the inside arch shape. Join these together with 2 in. x 1 in. batons. Attach hardboard over this former to make it rigid, and place it in between walls with brick supports underneath. Next, place in position the steel framework that will take up the thrust of the arch. There should be one angle iron at each corner with ties across them to brace the whole structure. Having done this you can proceed to lay up the arch in the same way as the walls, making sure that the joints are broken and, finally, that the centre course of wedges fits as tightly and neatly as possible. Use a brick hammer and wooden block to drive this last course well home.

When you have completed this brickwork, check that the iron

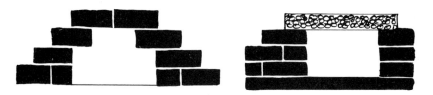

Fig. 27 A corbelled arch and a cast arch.

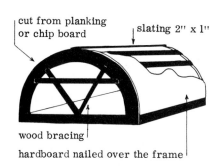

cut from planking or chip board

slating 2" x 1"

Fig. 28 An arch former showing its construction.

wood bracing

hardboard nailed over the frame

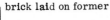
brick laid on former

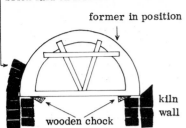

former in position

Fig. 29 An arch former in position.

kiln
wall

wooden chock

brick supports dismantled for
removing arch former

bracing is ready to take the strain before knocking out the
supports and removing the arch former. In the case of the
catenary arch, which is self-supporting, no steel braces will be
needed, so the former can be removed as soon as the arch is
completed. (See Rhodes *Kilns*, page 109 for catenary arch
calculation and construction details.) When using castable
refractory for a kiln arch, the procedure is the same as when
using bricks. The arch can be cast in one piece, or separated into
blocks (useful if you intend to pre-fire them in another kiln).
Cast the first piece in position separated by thin cardboard from
the next section, and then continue until the former is covered.
When the blocks have set they can be removed and fired separately, then replaced in position on the former and mortared in.
The former is then removed in the usual way as with brick
arches.

One advantage with this system of casting blocks is that the
former can be replaced at some later date and the arch dismantled
without damaging the blocks. A monolithic arch cast in one piece
is not an easy job to remove or replace elsewhere.

5 Insulation

The insulating blocks should have been built along with the rest
of the kiln walls (see Chapter 4) so it only remains to cover the
dome with a loose fill of whatever you intend to use as an
insulating material.

6 Damper and flue box

The flue box from the kiln wall to the chimney should be kept
as short as possible so that the efficiency of the chimney is not

impaired by excessive horizontal pull. The construction should be of solid fire brick, incorporating the damper slot: take care that the damper plate fits well.

There are several methods of damper control, the simplest being a loose brick at the base of the chimney which is removed during the firing to cut down the pull on the chimney, thus helping a reduction atmosphere in the kiln. A further advantage of this loose brick method is that a fire can be lit in the chimney base to preheat the stack in the early stages of firing; this will induce a stronger draught. The damper plate helps adjust the pull in the chimney, preventing cold air being drawn into the chamber through the fire mouths both during and after firing, when a slow cooling down is required.

A side damper in the flue box is an easy one to use since it needs no peg to keep it in position. I have also found that a damper made from a suitable kiln shelf will last longer than a metal plate, which may warp with the heat: this is very annoying if the plate locks in position during the course of a firing.

7 Chimney

The chimney should be of fire brick for the first ten feet or so,

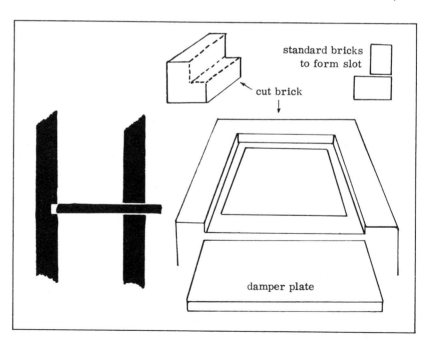

Fig. 30 The construction of a horizontal damper.

standard bricks to form slot

cut brick

damper plate

then either common brick, flue liners or asbestos pipe for the rest of the structure. Take care to build an upright and straight structure, and to provide adequate insulation should the chimney pass through the roof at any point. Asbestos tube should be supported with a tie rod down the back attached to the tube with wire rope. The base of this rod should be concreted into the foundation so that there is no likelihood of the chimney coming down in a gale.

8 Iron work and extras

Two or three inch medium weight angle iron should be adequate for most framework, bolted or welded in position with adjustable tie rods or chains crossing from corner to corner. Scaffolding poles with standard fittings can be used in the case of a large kiln. Bagwalls should be of loose structure for ease of adjustment when required, as it may be necessary to raise or lower them to get an even firing pattern.

Painting the inside of the chamber with glaze helps to bind up any small cracks or loose pieces of mortar, and when firing, this helps considerably to reflect the radiated heat back from the shiny reflective surface.

I have found it worth while to incorporate a small mouse hole in the collecting flue opposite the chimney flue exit. This is useful for cutting down the pull in the chimney, but is small enough not to act as a full damper. It allows the potter to let air in below the setting and helps unburnt gases clear themselves before going up the chimney (useful in view of present-day pollution).

Even when all factors of design and fuel, etc., have been thoughtfully worked out and the kiln carefully built according to the best known methods, it may not fire too well the first few times. Be patient, and with a few adjustments success should follow. After several firings most of the usual teething troubles should disappear.

Perhaps you will have more success than Bernard Palissy!

'I then painted my vessels with that compound, stacked them neatly in my kiln, and started my fire by the two openings. But my best efforts came to naught; for, though I watched over the kiln six days and nights, without sleep, almost without food, feeding the fire by the two openings, that glaze did not melt.'

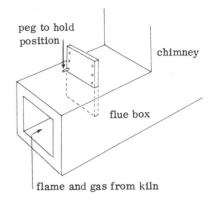

Fig. 31 The construction of a vertical damper.

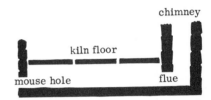

Fig. 32 Diagram of a mouse hole.

6 Kiln Log Extract

This was the thirteenth large salt firing, on Wednesday 4 December 1974. The kiln was fairly tightly packed, especially up over bagwall door side. All shelves had been washed with alumina hydrate.

Time	Pyro-meter reading	Notes
9.30 am	0°C	Lit up oil and air low. Good initial climb.
11.30 am	240°C	Temp same at this time last firing.
1.00 pm	380°C	Turned oil up.
2.00 pm	400°C	Second burner on low: damper full out.
2.30 pm	480°C	Up both oil lines.
3.00 pm	520°C	
5.00 pm	670°C	Slowing down after good start.
6.10 pm	790°C	
7.30 pm	920°C	Weather turning cold.
7.40 pm	940°C	Adding wood. Damper full out.
8.00 pm	980°C	
9.00 pm	1060°C	
9.30 pm	1100°C	Reduction starting: closed off secondary air and clammed up spies as cone 01 well down.
10.15 pm	1120°C	Good reduction: all's well.
11.30 pm	1180°C	Kiln seems to be sticking: cannot get climb. Noticed that damper has broken: this may have fallen down into the flue causing restriction on the chimney pull.
11.50 pm	1180°C	Still holding!

Time	Pyrometer reading	Notes
12.00 am	1190°C	
1.00 am	1190°C	Looks like we won't make it! What's happened? I'm sure the broken damper's done it.
2.00 am	1200°C	Moving very slowly. Opened up all ports and more frequent stoking. It's very cold tonight.
2.30 am	1230°C	Kiln seems to be climbing again. Began salting, 20 lb over the next hour.
3.30 am	1260°C	Cone 7 going well over. Oxidising to clean up for soak. (Vicar's cockerel crowing $2\frac{1}{2}$ hours before dawn, idiot!)
3.40 am	1280°C	Bagwall collapsed! It must have melted from salt attack: should have checked it. Pots rolled out of the fire mouth! Dowsed in bucket of water. What's happened? Stopped stoking and clammed up.

Drew kiln, and as I expected the bagwall was down and had knocked over one bank of shelves, bringing pots out of the fire mouth. All the rest of the kiln was okay. The damper had fallen in and blocked flues: must check plate before each firing. It always pays to check floor supports before a firing. I'm sure these were weakened by salt and slag attack from previous firings.

Bank Kiln

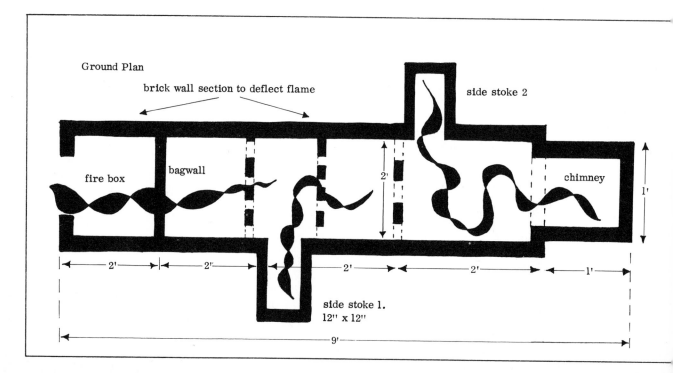

Ground Plan

brick wall section to deflect flame

fire box

bagwall

side stoke 2

chimney

2'

2'

2'

2'

2'

1'

1'

side stoke 1.
12" x 12"

9'

This bank kiln based on the Japanese Tamba kilns works well for small projects and experiments, especially at colleges. It can be built and fired without the bagwalls, using it as a simple open tube. The fire boxes at the side can be done away with in a simple version, but they do allow for a more even firing by equalising temperature above the main fire box.

1. Dig a trench of adequate size in the bank.
2. Line it with brick or clay to form the walls, fire box, chimney and bagwalls.
3. Use large slabs to cover the top of the trench after loading and seal the cracks with fine clay mix. Old galvanized iron sheets covered with earth will serve as covers for the top at low temperatures.

A chimney height of 6′ should be adequate, depending on the angle of the slope. The floor of the trench should be cut in steps to facilitate the placing of the pots. Slabs can be cast from ciment fondu for more permanent use. Start with a small fire so that the kiln doesn't heat up too fast at the fire box end.

Side Plan

2′

fire box

1′

9″

2′

side stoke

41

Wood Fired Raku Kiln

This small raku kiln can be constructed from any type of brick and fired with wood to temperature in six hours: to maintain a good working temperature, steady stoking is needed. Keep the door closed as much as possible to keep the chamber temperature steady. Should too strong a draught develop, pulling the flame through too fast, an old kiln shelf placed on top of the chimney will reduce the pull. Galvanised pipe can be used to extend the chimney height if the draught needs to be improved. A vacuum cleaner can be used as a blower to help produce a hot flame, as in a blacksmith's forge.

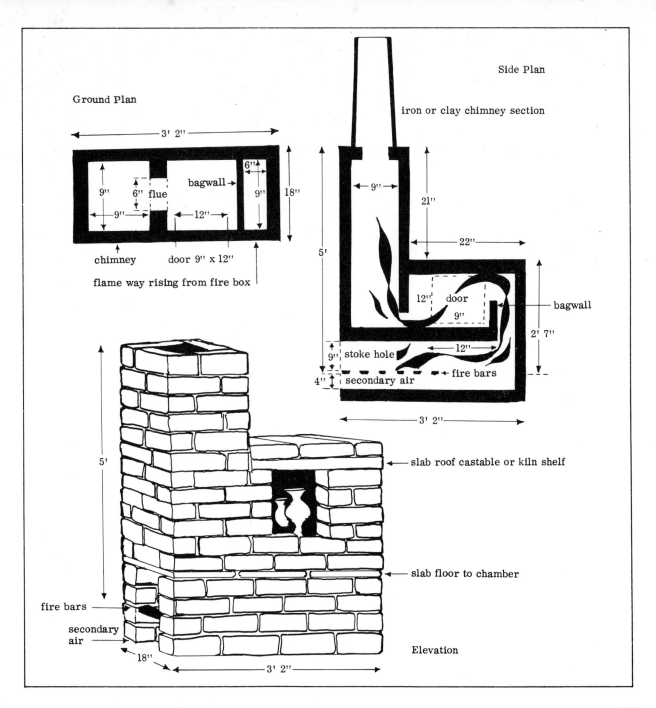

Ground Plan

3' 2"

9"

6" flue

6"

bagwall →

9"

18"

9"

12"

chimney

door 9" x 12"

flame way rising from fire box

Side Plan

iron or clay chimney section

9"

21"

22"

5'

12"   door

9"

bagwall

2' 7"

9"   stoke hole

12"

fire bars

4"   secondary air

3' 2"

5'

slab roof castable or kiln shelf

slab floor to chamber

fire bars

secondary air

18"

3' 2"

Elevation

43

Two raku kilns built by Alan
Wallwork.

Small Salt Kiln

The plans here are as for my own salt kiln which is fired with oil. There is a tendency for cold spots to develop just beside the burner ports: this trouble can be overcome by dampering back at top temperature a little and giving a good soak at cone 9—10. Twenty pounds of salt over the first firing developed a good cover over the chamber and by the sixth firing the amount of salt needed was down to seven pounds. The approximate time for firing from cold to cone 10 is nine hours.

Elevation

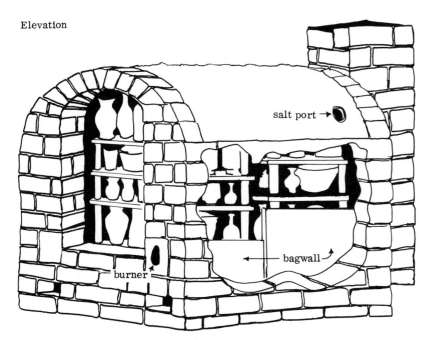

salt port →

← bagwall →

burner

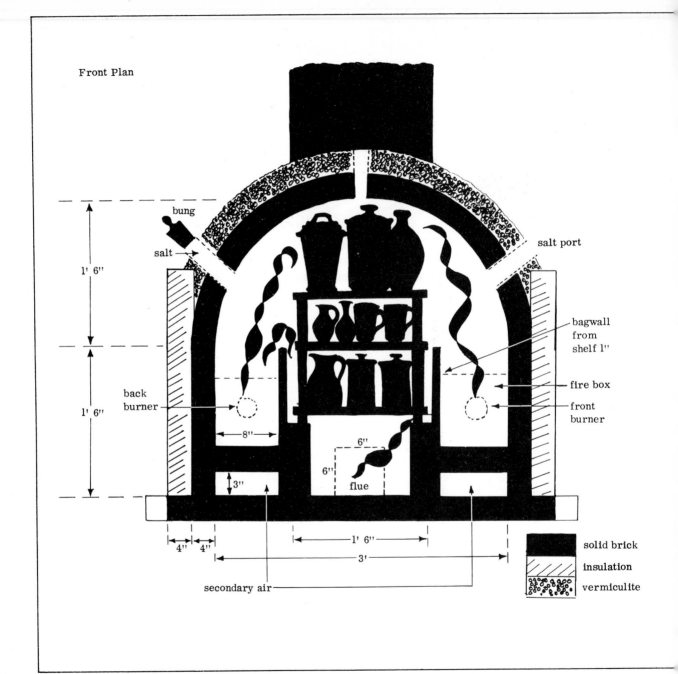

Front Plan

bung

salt

1' 6"

1' 6"

back
burner

salt port

bagwall
from
shelf 1"

fire box

front
burner

8"

6"

6"

3"

flue

4" 4"

1' 6"

3'

secondary air

solid brick

insulation

vermiculite

46

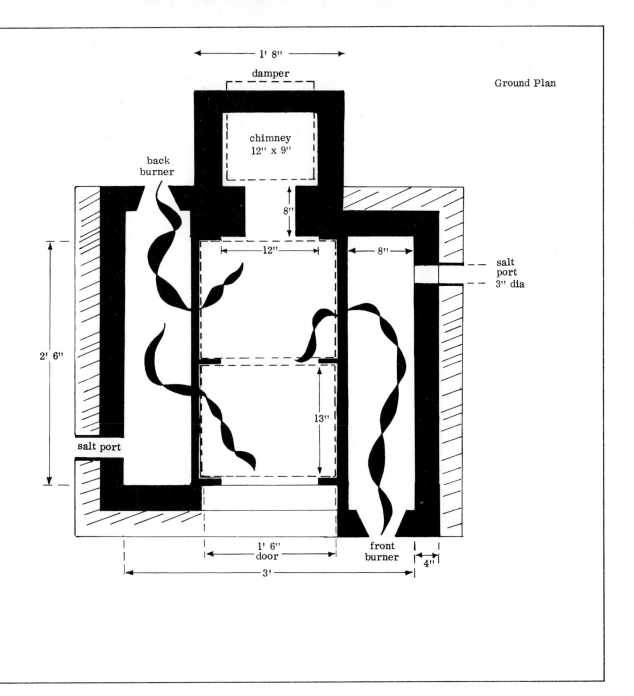

1' 8"

damper

chimney
12" x 9"

back
burner

8"

12"

8"

salt
port
3" dia

2' 6"

salt port

13"

front
burner

1' 6"
door

3'

4"

Right: Front view construction detail.

Below: Back view that shows the flue exit to the chimney.

The foundations and walls almost
ready for casting the arch.

Above: A Simple and effective
cube-shaped salt kiln, showing
angle iron supports and heavy
alumina resist on the inside of the
chamber. This example is from
Harrow College of Art.

Above: A good example of the
way that salting begins its vicious
attack on bricks.

Left: Cones are salted during a
firing and cannot always be relied
upon to give accurate temperature
readings.

Coal Fired Up-draught Kiln

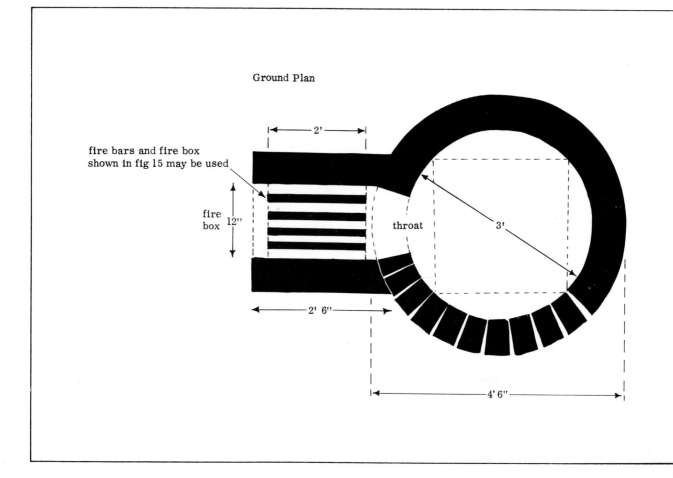

Ground Plan

fire bars and fire box
shown in fig 15 may be used

fire
box   12"

2'

throat

3'

2' 6"

4' 6"

This kiln needs several firings to reveal its behaviour pattern. An open placing with saggars on the floor and upper part of the setting will help even up the temperature from front to back. The floor area will fire hotter than the chimney, so in a glost firing glazes will have to be selected for temperature variation. Some very nice earthenware flower pots with soft flame flashes can be achieved, especially if wood is used once the pots have passed the water evaporation stage.

Common brick or solid fire brick can be used for construction at earthenware temperatures. I wouldn't recommend this kiln for temperatures higher than 1150°C, as considerable heat loss is likely, due to lack of insulation and over-firing of the floor area.

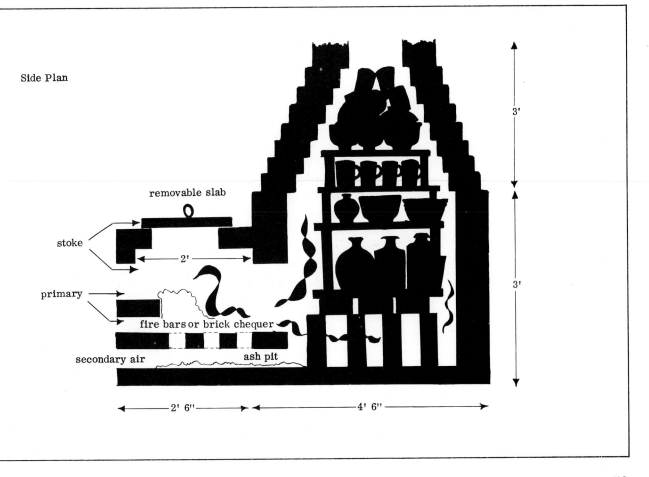

Side Plan

removable slab

stoke

2'

primary

fire bars or brick chequer

secondary air   ash pit

2' 6"   4' 6"

3'

3'

Peter Dick shows the floor plan
using common bricks set for round
chamber.

The coal kiln bricked up to the chimney level where the kiln walls close in the form of a bottle shape.

Inside the chamber showing the
floor bricks set in position and the
throat to the fire box.

Far left: Front view of a coal fire box from an old salt bottle kiln.

Left: The same kiln showing deterioration from salting inside.

Detail of an old coal bottle kiln fire box.

Catenary Kiln, Wood

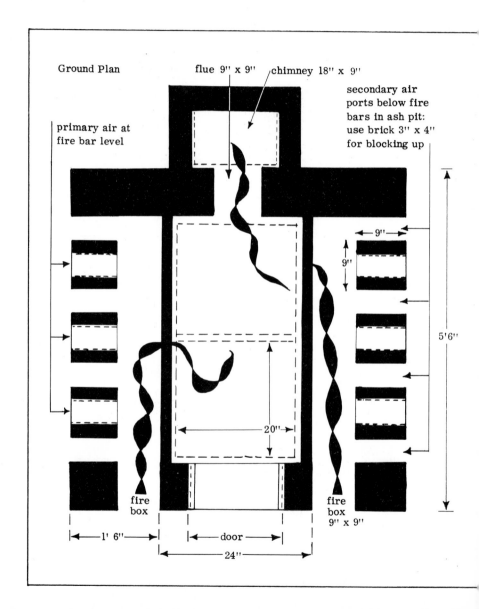

Ground Plan

flue 9" x 9" chimney 18" x 9"

secondary air ports below fire bars in ash pit: use brick 3" x 4" for blocking up

primary air at fire bar level

9"

9"

5'6"

20"

fire box

fire box 9" x 9"

1' 6"

door

24"

Careful packing and control of the primary and secondary air ports will help the logs burn evenly in these long fire boxes, allowing air in where combustion is weakest. A long poker will help to clear embers where necessary. Cone 8—9 should take 14 hours in a raw pot firing, using a maximum of one cord of wood that has been well seasoned.

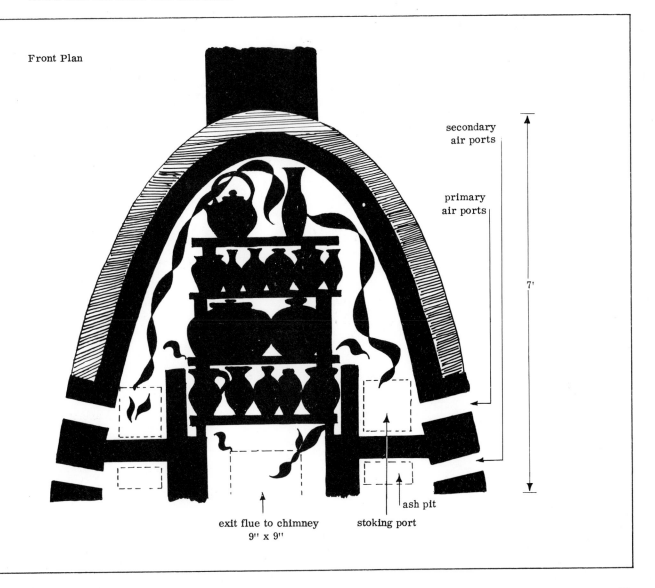

Front Plan

secondary air ports

primary air ports

7'

exit flue to chimney
9" x 9"

stoking port

ash pit

Elevation

primary
air

stoke ports   ash pit   secondary air 3" x 4"

Below: A view into John Maltby's
kiln with shelves in position.

Below centre: Neat kiln door
brickwork on John Maltby's
kiln.

Below right: Detail of chimney
flashing on Alan Wallwork's wood
kiln.

60

Front view of Alan Wallwork's
wood kiln when being drawn.
Note that door bricks are
numbered to facilitate blocking up.

An oil fired catenary kiln from
Harrow College of Art.

A shallow catenary kiln from Harrow College of Art. Note that the arch is beginning to collapse.

Gas Fired Car Kiln

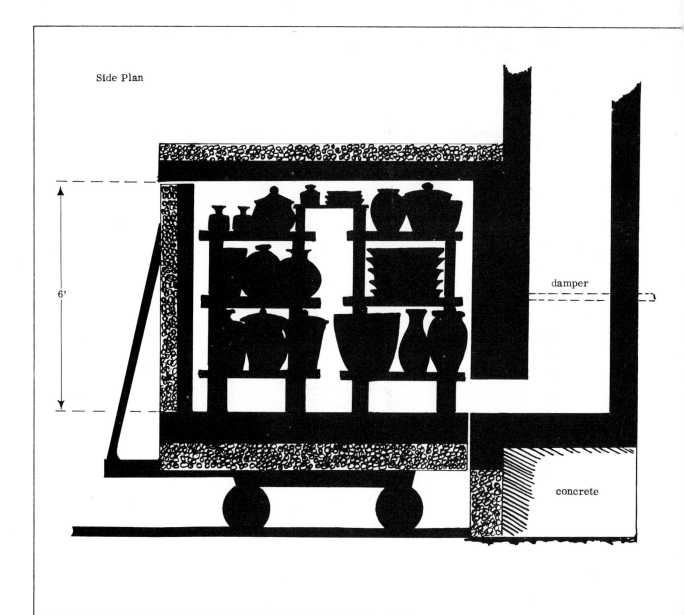

Side Plan

6'

damper

concrete

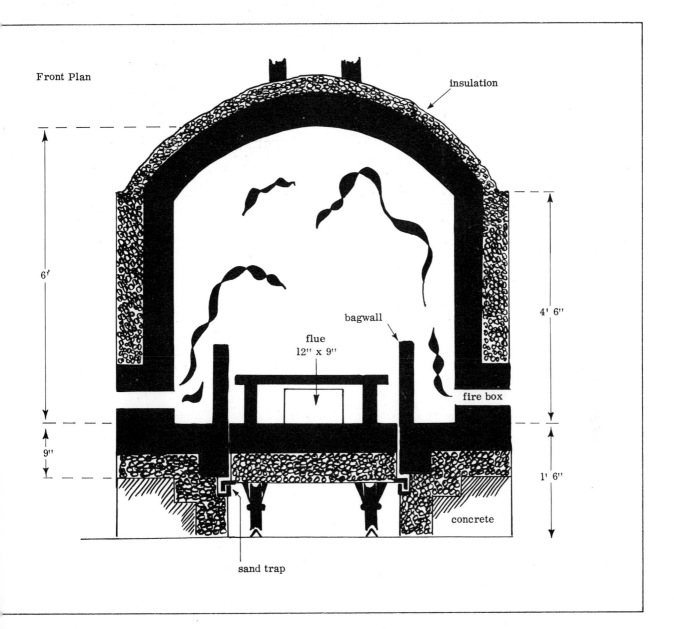

Front Plan

insulation

6'

4' 6''

9''

1' 6''

flue
12'' x 9''

bagwall

fire box

concrete

sand trap

Right: Detail of car track and wheel mountings and sand trap. Ensure that all iron work is soundly joined. A local blacksmith will quote for car construction if you give him a sensible working drawing. I have used pulley blocks as shown for wheels, but heavy cast iron ones are better if you can find them.

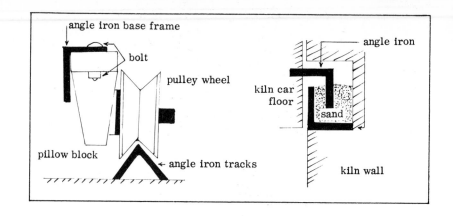

Ground Plan

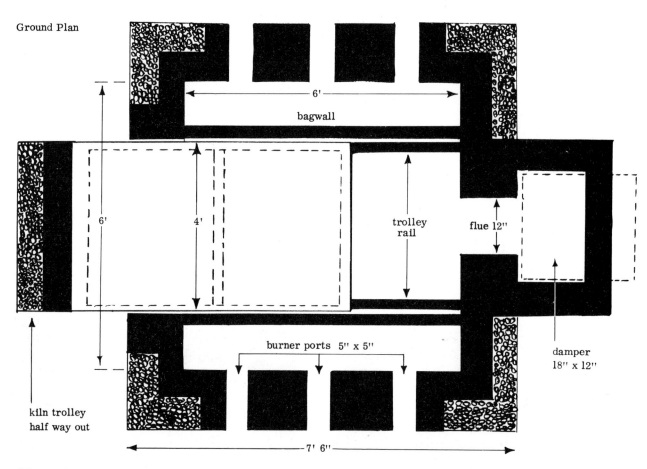

6'

bagwall

6'

4'

trolley rail

flue 12"

damper 18" x 12"

burner ports 5" x 5"

kiln trolley half way out

7' 6"

Below left: Detail of the oil fired car kiln at Dartington Hall workshop, showing flue and bagwall construction.

Below: Brickwork detail on the car at the Dartington Hall kiln.

Left: Detail of bagwall assembly and flue floor at Dartington Hall.

Front view of Muffy Anderson's propane fired kiln at Sebastopol, California. The particulars of this kiln are firstly, construction: hard brick on the outside and the first four courses, floor and sub-floor. Soft insulating brick for the lining, and a soft brick arch covered with castable refractory and tin as its outside. It has four high pressure propane burners: 200 000 BTU per burner, with two flues. There is maybe $\frac{1}{2}$ cone difference from top to bottom. The shelves are of silicon carbide and were rejects from a porcelain plant and a tile factory. The firing cycle for a bisque is an overnight soak and then 10 slow hours. Glazing to cone 9–10 is about 10 hours.

Gas burners in position on Muffy Anderson's kiln.

Two-chamber Salt Kiln

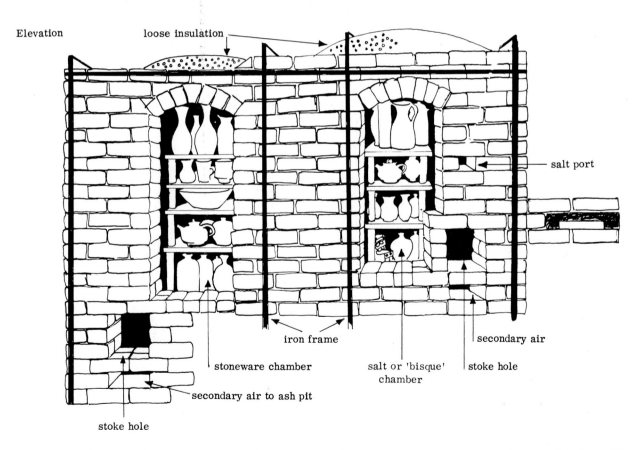

Elevation

loose insulation

salt port

iron frame

stoneware chamber

salt or 'bisque' chamber

secondary air

stoke hole

secondary air to ash pit

stoke hole

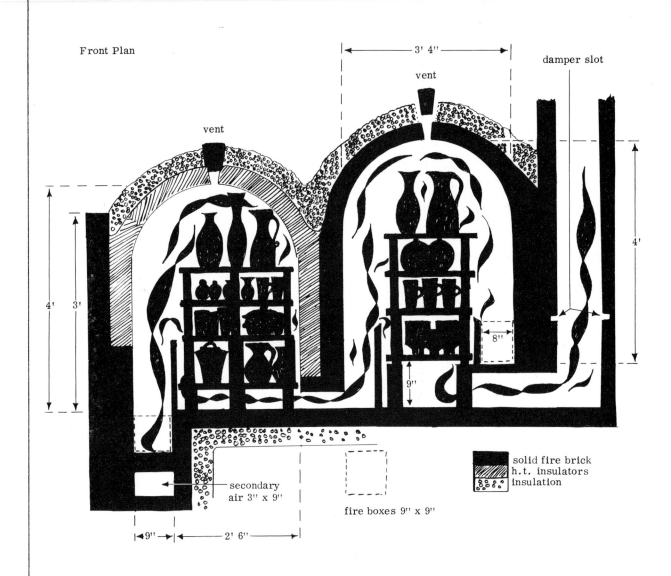

Front Plan

3' 4"

vent

damper slot

vent

4'

4'

3'

8"

9"

secondary
air 3" x 9"

fire boxes 9" x 9"

solid fire brick
h.t. insulators
insulation

9"

2' 6"

Ground Plan

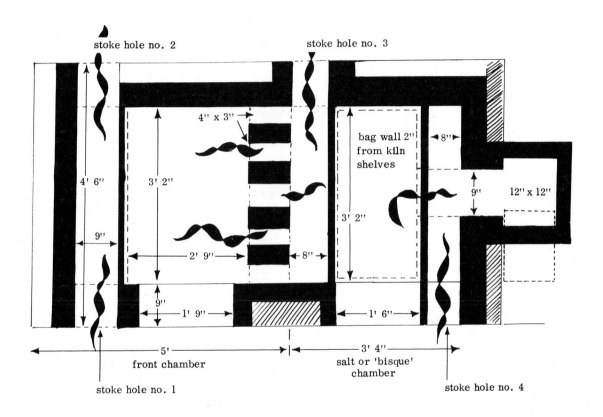

stoke hole no. 2

stoke hole no. 3

4" x 3"

bag wall 2"
from kiln
shelves

8"

4' 6"

3' 2"

9"

3' 2"

12" x 12"

9"

2' 9"

8"

9"

1' 9"

1' 6"

5'

front chamber

3' 4"

salt or 'bisque'
chamber

stoke hole no. 1

stoke hole no. 4

A two-chamber cross-draught and down-draught kiln that can be fired in four ways:

1 With wood or oil and a bisque firing in both chambers.
2 With the first chamber for reduced stoneware and a bisque from waste heat in the second.
3 Reduced or oxidising firing in the first chamber and a salt firing in the second. The salt firing is fine so long as the chamber is built from solid fire brick as shown in the plan.
4 Firing the second chamber only: this will mean that the linking ports from the first chamber will need to be blocked off with loose fire brick and fire clay and sand mortar at 3:1.
This kiln is a multi-purpose kiln that I have now used for 4 years with over a hundred firings. The chimney height of 18 feet is sufficient for both wood and oil fired from both chambers.

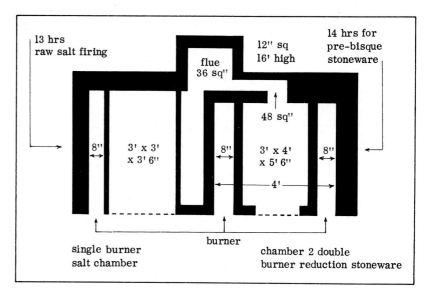

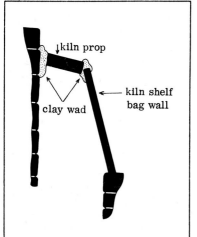

Left: An example of how a kiln-shelf can be used, when supported as a bagwall. However it is much better to use a more stable structure: soap bricks are ideal for this purpose as they are narrow and so don't take up too much valuable kiln space.

Above: John Maltby's two chamber kiln.

Opposite: These are the rough foundations laid out before building starts on a two-chamber kiln.

Inside a chamber: the arch has been cast from alumina cement to resist attack from salting. A high alumina batwash has been coated on all surfaces to give all-over protection and ensure a longer kiln life. However, a heavily salted interior gives much better salting to the pots.

Left: The swirlamiser oil burner in position.

Overleaf: The loose fill can be seen on the top of this chamber. This kiln has been fired many times and although it has settled (there are small cracks), it is still firing very well and has much life left in it even with persistent salting.

Overleaf opposite: Front view of the same kiln.

Appendices

Appendix 1 Suppliers List

UK suppliers

Clays, glazes and pottery supplies
Podmore and Son Ltd., Shelton, Stoke, Staffs. Tel. 0782-24571
The Fulham Pottery Ltd., 210 New King's Road, London SW6.
  Tel. 01-736-1188
Potclays Ltd., Brickkiln Lane, Etruria, Stoke, Staffs. Tel. 0782-
  29816
Ferro (GB) Ltd., Wombourne, Wolverhampton, Staffs.
  Tel. 09077-4144
Harrison Mayer Ltd., Meir, Stoke, Staffs. Tel. 0782-31611
Wengers Ltd., Etruria, Stoke, Staffs. Tel. 0782-25126

Bricks and castables
Gibbons Refractories Ltd., P O Box 19, Dudley, W. Midlands.
  Tel: 0384-53251
Sillbond Refractories Ltd., Herries Road, Sheffield 6.
  Tel. 0742-348074
Morganite Refractories Ltd., Neston, Wirral, Cheshire. Tel. 051-
  336-3911

Wheels
J W Ratcliffe and Sons, Old Boro Works, Rope Street, Shelton
  New Road, Stoke. Tel. 0782-611321

Ceramic fibre
Fiberfrax Carborundum, Carborundum & Co Ltd., Mill Lane,
  Rainford, St Helens, Lancs. Tel. 074-488-2941

Oil burners

Auto Combustion, Harcourt, Halesfield 13, Telford, Salop.
Tel. 0952-585574

Nu-way Air and Gas Mixers, P O Box 14, Berry Hill, Droitwich,
Worcs. Tel. 09057-4244

Oil kilns

Midland Monolithic Furnace Lining Co. Ltd., Barwell, Leics.
Tel. 0455-42061

Gas kilns and installations

Bricesco Kilns, Bricesco House, Park Avenue, Woolstanton,
Newcastle-under-Lyme, Staffs.

Fire Gas Kilns Ltd., Newstead Trading Estate, Trentham, Stoke,
Staffs. Tel. 0782-23641

Kilns and Furnaces Ltd., Keele Street Works, Tunstall, Stoke,
Staffs. Tel. 0782-84642

US suppliers

Burners and parts

Flynn Burner Corp., 425 Fifth Ave, New Rochelle, N.Y. 10802

Johnson Gas Appliance Co., Cedar Rapids, Iowa 52405

Maxon Corp., 201 E. 18th St., Muncie, Ind. 47302

Mine & Smelter Industries (formerly DFC Corp.) P.O. Box 16607,
Denver, Colo. 80216

Pyronics Inc., 17700 Miles Ave., Cleveland, Ohio 44128

Ransome Gas Industries Inc., 2050 Farallon Drive, San Leandro,
Calif. 94577

Pottery material suppliers

American Art Clay Co. Inc., 4717 W. 16th St., Indianapolis, Ind.
46222

Cedar Heights Clay Co., 50 Portsmouth Road, Oak Hill, Ohio
45656

Creek Turn Pottery Supply, Route 38, Hainesport, N.J. 08036

Hammill & Gillespie Inc., 225 Broadway, New York, N.Y.
10007

Minnesota Clay, 8001 Grand Ave. So., Bloomington, Minn.
55420

The Monomy Potter's Supply Co., RFD 140E, Chatham, Mass.
02633

Newton Potters Supply Inc., 96 Rumford Ave., Box 96,
Newton, Mass. 02165

Rovin Ceramics and Pottery, 6912 Schaefer Road, Dearborn,
    Mich. 48216
The Salem Craftsmen's Guild, 3 Alvin Pl., Upper Montclair,
    N.J. 07043
Standard Ceramic Supply Co., Box 4435, Pittsburgh, Pa. 15205
Trinity Ceramic Supply Co., 9016 Diplomacy Row, Dallas,
    Texas 75235
Van Howe Co., 1185 S. Cherokee Avenue, Denver, Colo. 80223
Westwood Ceramic Supply Co., 14400 Lomitas Avenue, City of
    Industry, Calif. 91744

Refractory suppliers
Babcock & Wilcox Co., Refractories Div., 161 E. 42 Street, New
    York, N.Y. 10017
A. P. Green Co., 1018 E. Breckenridge Street, Mexico, Mo.
    65265
Carborundum Co., Refractories and Electronic Div., Box 337,
    Niagara Falls, N.Y. 14302
Denver Fire Clay Co., 2401 E. 40th Avenue, Box 5507, Denver
    Colo. 80217
Grefco Inc., 299 Park Avenue, New York, N.Y. 10017
Metropolitan Refractories, Tidewater Terminal, So. Kearny,
    N.J. 07032
New Castle Refractories, Box 471, New Castle, Pa. 16103
Norton Co., Industrial Ceramics Division, Worcester, Mass.
    01606
Pyro Engineering Corp., 200 S. Palm Avenue, Alhambra, Calif.
    91801

Appendix 2

Arch and radial brick formulae

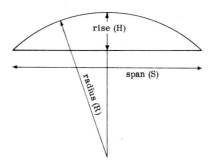

To find the Radius of an Arch when the rise and span are known:

$$R = \frac{\left(\dfrac{S}{2}\right) + H^2}{2H}$$

To find the Rise of an Arch when the radius and span are known:

$$H = R - \sqrt{R^2 - \left(\frac{S}{2}\right)^2}$$

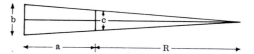

R = Inside radius of circle
a = Length of brick
b = Outside thickness of brick
c = Inside thickness of brick